Superhuman Mind Hacks

Live life of a superhuman, discover your full potential

AMARPREET SINGH

THE THOUGHT FLAME
TURNING SPARK INTO FLAME

info@thethoughtflame.com

www.thethoughtflame.com

Table of Contents

Introduction

Your brain is one of the most powerful computing devices ever known to mankind and the truth of the matter is that there are many people out there who will never actually learn how to utilize the fullest potential of their brain in regards to brain power.

In order to utilize the whole capacity of your brain you need to think of it as a muscle. In order to strengthen your muscle, you need to work it out. Just like any other muscles you need to constantly train it in order to strengthen it. The more you work it out, the more powerful it will become.

Since your brain is the most important part about you and it controls your every thought and feeling, strengthening your brain just makes sense. Your brain defies who you are as a person and it is a real shame that most people can go through your entire life without realizing how much potential their brain actually has.

Unfortunately today there is not enough emphasis placed on the importance of the brain and its overall health. In fact it is mostly ignored and overlooked when instead professionals are busy creating stimulation products such as the Internet and new TV's.

That is exactly what I am looking to change within this eBook. In this book your learn a variety of fun tips and techniques that will help you to supercharge your brain. In this book you will also find a variety of exercises that you can use to improve your memory, improve your knowledge case and help to keep your brain running light a finely tuned engine.

Remember, when you first begin to work out any part of your body, it takes time until it is as strong as you want it to be. With the exercises in this book you will need to work out your brain every day until you are able to utilize its full potential.

So, what are you waiting for? Let's get started!

Chapter One: The First Step To A Healthy Brain Is Having A Healthy Body

The first step that you will need to take in order to supercharge your brain, is to make sure you are eating and exercising properly. You need to think of your brain as a fine tuned engine on a sports car, such as a Lamborghini or Ferrari. These fast and powerful cars need premium fuel in order to run at their full potential. What do you think would happen if you put regular fuel in a Lamborghini?

The same scenario applies to your brain. You have this powerful computing device in your head, and in order for it to function properly, you need to provide it with the best fuel possible. Why would you want to slow it down and ruin it with junk food?(also known as a regular fuel). So the first step to supercharging your brain is to start with your diet.

The Diet To Having A Healthier Brain

The first step in creating a diet plan for your supercharged brain, is to cut out all fast food and junk food. This may be difficult to do for some people, but drinking soda and eating empty calories will have a negative effect on your body and your brain. The best advice we give to our students is to invest some time into learning how to cook. Learning how to cook will essentially kill two birds with one stone. You are going to be stimulating your mind with learning a new skill and developing a new hobby. You are also going to be eating healthier, which in turn will give your brain the proper high octane fuel that it needs to become supercharged. Once you have the junk food cut out of your diet, you can then move onto foods that will increase your brain and give it the power that it needs.

A Healthy Brain Requires More Energy Than You May Realize

Have you ever heard the fact that your brain only uses 20% of its caloric intake regardless of the fact that this number only represents a small percentage of your overall caloric intake for your entire body?

This fact goes to show you that if you are going to supercharge your brain, you are going to need to make sure it has the energy to perform throughout the day. The best way to make sure your brain is fully energized is to have brain friendly snack foods available throughout the day. The best snacks foods for your brain include:

- Pecans
- Berries
- Cashews
- Whole Grains
- Walnuts

I recommend that you keep these foods at your desk and periodically eat a few hand fulls and your brain will have all the energy it needs to stay powered up throughout the day.

Don't Forget To Keep Yourself Hydrated Throughout The Day

Now that you are making sure your brain remains at the proper energy levels throughout the day, the next step is to make sure that you are hydrated . Hydration is a key factor in achieving your brains full capability, and in order to make sure your brain is running at it's highest levels, you will need to drink between 2.2 and 3 liters of water a day.

Like our car analogy earlier, you need to think of water like the oil you put in your car. The oil keeps everything lubricated and working properly. If you are dehydrated or have not been drinking enough water your brain and body will slow down. So make sure you are drinking the recommended amount of water in addition to eating your brain foods.

Workout Your Body To Workout Your Mind

While correcting your diet will allow you the fuel to power to your brain, you will need to go one more step if you want to supercharge your brain. In order to maximize your brain functions, you will need to make sure your body is getting the proper daily exercise. Exercise helps the body for two main reasons:

1. The first reason is that exercise releases endorphins and chemicals that stimulate the body.

2. The second reason is that exercise can reduce stress, which has a big negative effect on overall brain health.

So in order to have a strong mind, you cannot forget to workout your body too.

So, what is the best way to strengthen your body and mind and where? There is no best place to do both then at the gym.

There are a variety of exercises and personal trainers that are willing to help you get into shape. Both men and women will see an immediate benefit in both brain activity and mental health after going to the gym for a few weeks. A simple routine of exercises that get your blood pumping for an hour will benefit your brain immensely. The endorphins and testosterone that will be released into your body have been shown to have a positive effect on your brain for up to forty eight hours.

In addition to going to the gym, there are exercises that you can do to stimulate your brain even further . Walking and running are both great forms of exercise that stimulate your brain at the same time. Have you ever had a long run and you are always thinking about new ideas and inventions? Some of the best inventors of our generations have experienced a breakthrough moment during a walk. Yoga and flexibility classes are also great for you brain. Increasing flexibility in a relaxed environment will lower your blood pressure and increase blood flow. Blood flow plays a big role in supercharging your brain, as you will need more oxygen and blood flowing to your brain.

Chapter Two: The Best Ways To Improve Your Mental Power

Now, the whole point of this book is to supercharge your brain, right? Well in order to do that there are many ways to achieve it and in this chapter you will find out exactly how to supercharge your way. In this chapter you will various techniques that you can use to supercharge your brain in the best way and how to apply those techniques in real time.

How To Improve Your Brain Power Through The Use of Experience

The next step in supercharging your brain, is to allow it to expand through different experiences. Allowing your brain to try new things and experience different settings and locations, will stimulate and allow your mind to grow. The best way to improve your mind through experiences is to travel to new locations. Even if you don't have the budget to travel around the world and visit different cultures, you can still travel and explore new locations near where you live. Just remember that the more foreign the location the more you will stimulate your mind.

How To Improve Your Brain Power Through The Use of Different Cultures

Experiencing different cultures and ways of life can not only stimulate your brain, it can change your entire mindset. While traveling around the world can be expensive and not everybody can afford it, we recommend that you try to save up and travel to a foreign location at least once in your life. The way your brain becomes stimulated is through the five senses; smell, sight, sound, taste and touch. The more senses you can stimulate at the same the time, the faster your brain will grow as well. This is the reason that visiting new countries and trying new things can speed up your supercharging process.

Nothing will expose all five of your senses to new stimulation better then visiting a new country. All your senses will be stimulated at the same time and your brain will be re-energized just trying to process all this information. Think about all the new things you can try and explore in a new country. The sights, the food, the different languages, all of these are great ways to stimulate your mind. This is why we advise parents to take their kids traveling to other countries when they are younger. The new sights and sounds of an unfamiliar country will allow them to not only broaden their horizon but also expand their mind.

Another great reason to travel, is to re-examine your perspective on life. Visiting third world countries will allow you to realize everything you take for granted living back home. While you are complaining about nothing being on TV, there are people who are trying just to survive. This can be a life changing perspective, which will allow you to prioritize your life and make sure you are taking advantage of every opportunity presented to you.

Improve Your Brain Power By Utilizing Your Taste Buds

Another great way to stimulate your senses is through acquiring new tastes in different food.

The sense of taste is one of the most powerful senses you have. Having a pleasant taste will set off numerous chemical reactions in your brain releasing all kinds of different chemicals. The reason for our brain rewarding us for eating comes from our days as hunters.

Back when we had to hunt for our food, we didn't know when the next meal would come. So our brains made sure we had the proper motivation by releasing endorphins into our body once we ate our kill. These endorphins reminded us how much we loved eating, and these same endorphins are still released when we eat today. Think about a time when you had a great meal. How relaxed and satisfied you felt after eating . The reason you felt that way was due to the release of endorphins. So in order to stimulate your sense of taste you should be trying out new and different types of food.

Some foods you may like, some you may hate,

but the point is all the same, your brain will be stimulated. Try taking new cooking classes or food tasting groups. With Groupon and other half off discount services, you can try new restaurants out each week for half the price. So make it a priority to try out new foods around your local area.

Chapter Three: The Art of Mindfulness

Today we all live in an extremely busy world where we are constantly faced with the task of devoting all of our attention to multiple things at once. Let's face it, many of us today plan our days while we are on the way to work or simply wing it. We are often rushes to complete many tasks and the many things that we have to do that it can sometimes be extremely difficult to balance our lives appropriately.

You may fit into this category then the chances are that you have lost touch with life in the present. Just think about it. Have you ever stopped to think of how you felt every morning when you wake up or are you the type of person that immediately jumps into doing things right away the moment you crawl out of bed? Or do you even remember any small details that you do, think or feel throughout your busy day?

Being out of touch with the present can cause you to forget what is truly happening in your life. This is where the art of mindfulness can come into play.

What Is Mindfulness Anyway?

Mindfulness is the practice of proactively devoting your undivided attention to the present moment at all times while accepting everything that happens without any form of judgment. Mindfulness has been used by many cultures and religions through human history to remarkable success . Heck, most religions come with some form of prayer technique or meditation practice. This same practice has been brought into mainstream medicine in more convenient ways. Practicing mindfulness has a lot of advantages that it can add to your life – both physical and psychological.

Not only will it give you a more satisfied life by helping you get the most from enjoyable moments, but being mindful will:

- Relieve your stress
- Lower your blood pressure, which can improve the overall health of your heart.
- Has shown signs of reducing chronic pain
- Improve your sleeping habits
- Improve your overall mental health

Just think about it. If you are having a conversation with a colleague and are focusing your undivided attention on that conversation, then you are more likely to remember more details than if you were thinking about what movie to catch that weekend. It makes perfect sense.

Some experts even believe that practicing mindfulness can help people accept their life's experiences rather than simply reacting to them. There is no doubt that practicing mindfulness will have a positive effect on your life. The concept is easier than the execution though. There are so many distractions that can easily pull you from this zone . As with anything worth doing, adapting this practice will take time.

Techniques To Use To Become Mindful

There is certainly more than one way to practice mindfulness so they are not limited to what's mentioned in this book. Just remember that the goal of mindfulness is to keep yourself in a constant state of alert by focusing on your thoughts and emotions all of the time without any form of judgment. Accomplishing this will refocus your mind to always being in the moment instead of wondering aimlessly.

Start off by paying attention to subtle body sensations like itching or tingling but do so without judgment. In other words, don't think of them as irritating. Instead , just notice that they are happening and let them pass. This is a practice that hones your instincts to interact without judgment.

Pay attention to all of your senses. When you smell, see, taste, feel, or hear something , pay attention to it but only focus on the sense. The same goes with your emotions. Allow your emotions to be present but instead of reacting to them, simply acknowledge the emotion without judgment. By learning to control your emotions and senses, you will pay closer attention to other details instead of being distracted by your senses.

How Meditation Can Help Unlock Your Mindful Nature

Meditation is probably one of the best techniques available for practicing mindfulness. Choose a time every day that you can sit in solitude. Sit quietly and focus on your breathing. As thoughts come to you, let them pass without judgment. Once they have passed, continue focusing on your breaths.

Cultivating your mindfulness begins with meditation. As you learn to focus your mind during these sessions, you will naturally begin to develop a systematic approach to focusing your mind. Even fifteen minutes of meditation per day can improve your entire life.

It's not a hard skill to learn but it does require a great deal of patience. For some, it's best to follow instructions or listen to tapes. Others might need to add in the extra benefit of support from a group or instructor since these help keep you motivated. Just be sure that if you seek support , that those you group with all share the same beliefs and goals as you.

How To Start Becoming Mindful Today

Most meditation practices revolve around learning to concentrate by using breathing as a focal point to this concentration. When thoughts inevitably pop into your mind, you will learn to simply let them happen without any sort of judgment. The most popular form of meditation is probably yoga, which has the added bonus of reducing the body's resistance to stress. It doesn't really matter what practice you choose to incorporate, so long as it accomplishes the important goal of helping you to live in the moment rather than letting your thoughts dictate your actions. Remember, we are doing this to help us become less forgetful. With that end goal in mind, here is what you should accomplish:

1. Go With The Flow-As you meditate more, you will establish the ability to focus on every detail. This will allow you to retain much more information than if you let your mind wonder hopelessly. We cannot stop thoughts from randomly popping into our heads. What we can control is whether or not we judge these thoughts. Don't think of them as good or bad – rather, think of them as something that just happens.

2. Pay Attention To Everything That Happens Around You-The real challenge comes from learning not to latch onto a single emotion or sensation. For example, if you are stressed because you are behind at work, this stress might eat at you all throughout the entire day. So when you should be listening to your spouse about an important event, you might be focused on this stress instead. That leads you to forgetting whatever important event was being told to you because you weren't paying attention in the first place!

3. Don't Forget To Stick With It-In the beginning, there will be times when meditation doesn't seem relaxing at all. It gets easier over time and you will become happier as your self-awareness allows you to enjoy every single moment in life.

4. Never Give Up-Even if you happen to miss a meditation session then you should not worry. Instead, pick it back up the following day. So many people will miss one session, get bummed out and then stop. It's not a big deal if you happen to miss it. Be persistent and never give up!

5. Accept What Is-Paying attention is just not enough; you will also need to accept it without any form of judgment. Acceptance starts with redirecting your thoughts whenever your mind wonders. For most of us, this means that our mind wonders into planning, daydreaming, and even criticism of ourselves. When you notice these thoughts, gently redirect them back into the present.

Chapter Four: The Dangers of Forgetfulness

Do you find yourself forgetting where you put the keys? Maybe your mind feels like it shuts down early in the afternoon? One of the leading causes of forgetfulness is the sheer amount of information that people are forced to process each day. We live in a world of information overload. It starts at an early age too. In school, kids are given a ton of information in very short periods of time. Then they must process and memorize this information in order to pass an exam. So we are taught our whole lives that in order to be successful, we must process and store as much information as possible. That's the world we live in – the age of information overload.

It's no wonder that we tend to forget certain things. Our brains are only capable of retaining so much information at a time. The fact that we are forced to use this information to make important decisions means that we cannot avoid it. The overwhelming amount of information that we receive causes our minds to become exhausted well before the end of the day. An exhausted mind becomes a forgetful one.

Our brains are still wired to deal with problems that were present thousands of years ago. They have not caught up to our current lifestyle so it's no wonder that being exposed to all of this information causes lapses in our memory. The problem is that people have trouble separating relevant data from irrelevant data at the speed, which it's being thrown at them. It strains the brain and leads to fatigue, which ultimately leads to forgetfulness. The problem is that information overload can't be avoided in today's world because it has become such a normal part of everyday life.

I have some great news for you. Even though it might be impossible to avoid information overload, it's possible to regain control of your mind! This can be accomplished by organizing information into a way that optimizes your brain's efficiency. In essence, you can control the amount of information that your brain is forced to process. Best yet, it's a lot easier than you might believe.

Try Writing Down Your Tasks As Often As Possible

Many people boast about their ability to memorize their "to-do" lists. What they don't realize is that they are unknowingly overloading their brain with unnecessary information. Trying to memorize a list is not something to brag about. It's easy to fall prey to this bad habit since we are trained from childhood that memorizing information is directly linked to success. Free yourself from these bonds by externalizing as much information as possible.

If you find yourself trying to memorize your daily tasks, try writing them down instead. Anyone can memorize a list but it's those who learn to externalize who gain a huge advantage. Look at it logically.

How much of your brain capacity are you taking up if you are memorizing 20 tasks each day? How much unnecessary clutter will your mind have to sift through when trying to recall a memory or process new information? If you create lists instead of memorizing tasks, then you are essentially freeing up your brain to take on more important information.

By storing information in your head, your brain has a tough time focusing since it's using up all of its energy trying to recall these tasks that could have been externalized. Furthermore, writing a list manually enables muscle memory to help store the information in your brain. It's a win-win situation!

Here are some examples of information that can be externalized:

1. "To-Do" Lists

2. Reminders

3. Appointments

4. Exercise Appointments

5. Birthdays and Holidays

6. Your Work Schedule

Make Your Biggest and Toughest Decisions In The Morning

First of all, let's look at the neuroscience behind decision making. Every time your mind makes a decision, neuro-resources are used. It doesn't matter whether it's a big or small decision, all decisions use up these resources. Why does this matter? Well if you are making decisions as they come up, then you are not using these resources in an organized manner. This will cause your brain to become fatigued much too early in the day. Organizing your decision making will help keep your brain fresh throughout the remainder of the day. This will naturally cause you to become less forgetful.

Organize Your External Environment

Organizing your environment will lessen the burden on your mind. Disorganized individuals tend to be much more forgetful than those who are organized. The worst part is that so many wear their unhealthy disorganization habits as a badge of honor. They are happy about it until they misplace their keys or lose their phone. Then it becomes a nightmare.

Transform your physical environment into a series of reminders to help alleviate the need for your brain to remember things. By externalizing where everything is, you are creating less stress on having to remember where to find important items.

Stop Multitasking

How often do you check your email while talking on the phone? Or maybe you like to use meetings as a chance to catch up on texts? If you do this, then you've likely bragged about how you are a pro at multitasking. Well, I'm about to drop the cold, hard truth on you. Multitasking is a myth. The human mind cannot multitask; our brains simply are not capable of it.

When you're performing multiple tasks at the same time , your brain is not multitasking . It's shifting its attention from one task to another so rapidly that it might feel that you're doing it all at once, but you're really not. What society calls "multitasking" is actually fast-paced attention seesawing.

Rapidly swapping your focus depletes your brain's fuel supply (glucose). The result is that each time you swap your attention, your brain loses its ability to focus . So you are performing at subpar levels while adding much more stress to your brain. So it's no wonder that those who "multitask" tend to lose a lot of information. Simply put, they forget what they were doing and how they were doing it. They lose any important information about all of the tasks. So if they are asked to recall the process later, they have already forgotten . To be more precise, they never remembered it in the first place.

The solution is actually a simple one; focus on one task at a time. Once it's finished, then move onto the next. You will find that you get so much more accomplished while retaining the entire process.

Chapter Five: Using Games To Make You A Superhuman

We continue to talk about your brain as a muscle and different ways you can work it out and strengthen it. Games and mental challenges are great ways to make sure your brain gets its proper workout every day. Games are highly recommended in our game plan to supercharge your brain, for two distinct reasons. The first reason , there is a competitive nature to playing any type of game. Which if you remember, we mentioned how competitive activities spur faster brain growth.

The second reason is that games give you a way to measure your progress. Whether the game is skill based or timed, you can mark down your progress and try to improve each time that you play. We are going to list a few of our favorite games for improving your cognitive functions.

Try to time block an hour each day to practice these games and stimulate your brain.

Using Crossword Puzzles

The first games we are going to talk about are crossword puzzles. This word association game has been featured in newspapers for as long as they have been published. Cross word puzzles will test your creative thinking and memory skills. Your brain will be tested on trial and error skills as you try to figure out how to solve these puzzles. While the crossword puzzles in the paper may be too complex, feel free to start slow and download some easy ones on the internet. As you become more familiar with the clues and with your word solving skills, you will see you skill level improve and you can move up to more difficult puzzles.

Using Chess and Checkers

Chess and Checkers are great ways to improve your critical thinking skills and decision making skills. Checkers is an easier game to learn and play, but the stimulation on your brain is similar to chess. If you are looking for a more complicated game that requires more brain activity, learn how to play chess.

Chess requires you to plan ahead sometimes many moves out. You have to not only think about what you are going to do, but what your opponent is trying to do as well. This is some tough mental stimulation! If you want to take your game to the next level, look for local chess clubs in the area. These clubs cater to any skill level and discussing strategy with like minded individuals, will elevate your game to the next level.

Using Sodoku

Sudoku has risen in popularity over the past 10 years due to the puzzles ability to stimulate the left half of your brain. The left side of the brain is responsible for linear problem solving , which in this case is math related. Sudoku is easy to learn and puzzles can be completed in less than an hour. There are an endless amount of Sudoku puzzles online, each with a corresponding difficulty meter. This allows you to track your progress and make sure you are challenging your brain. Don't get discouraged if you hit a plateau. Just keep trying your best and really focusing. After a few weeks at that difficulty level, you will breakthrough and your brain will become even stronger.

Using Video Games

The last way to improve your mind that we are going to talk about, is through video games.

Now before you jump to conclusions , let us state that video games do mentally stimulate your mind. The problem with video games, is that users tend to only play video games and do nothing else to improve their mind.

It all comes down to playing video games in moderation. If you are spending eight hours a day in front of a TV playing video games and eating junk food, you are most likely not going to have a supercharged brain. New research has shown that video games do improve hand eye coordination and have been known to stimulate your mind. Just remember to maintain a balance in your life and make sure you get some fresh air every once in awhile.

Learning New Vocabulary

Another great way to expand your mind is through learning new vocabulary. Take time during the day to learn five new words and commit them to memory. Then test yourself daily on the words you learned the day before. Make sure are memorizing the words. Then challenge yourself to use those five words during a conversation. At the end of the week take your list of words and put them on flash cards and test yourself. See how many you remember and how many you actually used in some sort of conversation.

Using Creative Card Games

Strategy card games like poker and Black Jack can also improve your brain capacity. Now we are not advocating you go out and start gambling like crazy, just to supercharge your brain. But home poker games or black jack games with friends can be mentally stimulating and fun at the same time. Poker requires a strategy and the ability to read your opponents, which caters to the right side of your brain. Black jack is a game of quick math and addition, so it will strengthen the left side of your brain.

Chapter Six: Ways To Improve Your Brain Function Using The Art Neuroplasticity

For a long time , majority of us clung to the wrong notions about the human brain. This is because much of our knowledge about the brain is culled from conventional wisdom that is primarily based on the outdated scientific understandings of the 1950' s. As a result, we held on to a heap of faulty ideas for a long time - like 'our ability to learn or acquire new skills is bound to decline as we age'; 'our memory will progressively falter as we grow older'; 'the number of our brain cells decreases every year'; 'our IQ is set by the age of five and will remain constant at this level for the rest of our lives'.

Well, what used to be myth (neuroplasticity) is now the universal truth and what used to be the universal truth (all the faulty ideas above) is now myth . It has been proven over and over again by numerous contemporary studies that human intelligence is not fixed or static – it can be increased; that even the personality traits we have exhibited since childhood can be changed; that we can inject new life to an aging brain; that damaged or impaired brains can regain full functionality.

Neuroplasticity, the emerging science that has caught everyone's undivided attention lately, is making all these happen. The adage 'you can never teach an old dog new tricks' has become totally irrelevant because of this. Just like in the old times when people thought the earth was the center of the universe until Coppernicus proved this belief is wrong and changed everybody's perspective, the cumulative studies about the plasticity of the brain is drastically also changing our views about the brain and so we are starting to realize the awesome power of the brain to effect changes.

Here are some proven ways to enhance the power of your mind using the art of neuroplasticity.

Get Rid Of All Of Your Modern Gadgets

Modern gadgets such as calculators, translation software, spell-check and auto-correct applications may offer convenience but too much dependence on them leaves the corresponding brain synapses that used to do the work highly vulnerable to pruning since they will be rarely used – dulling your mind and diminishing your skill in that field as a consequence.

Be Open To New Experiences

The brain gets excited every time you engage in a new activity. A novel activity triggers the brain to release dopamine, which aside from being a neurotransmitter is also a trigger to motivate you and prepare you for learning. At the same time , the novel activity stimulates a flurry of successive brain processes. New synapses are created which build on each other to create more synaptic connections, which in turn also build more synaptic connections as the learning process for the novel activity is taking place.

Based on this, brain experts believe people with higher intelligence have developed and fortified more neural connections than people with average intelligence. In other words, the individual differences in intelligence can be traced to the number of synaptic connections made between neurons , how these connections affect subsequent connections, and how long these connections will last. By always being a knowledge junkie constantly in search of novel activities to engage with, you will be priming your brain for learning.

Never Stop Pushing Yourself

You need to keep your brain always on its toes so it won't stop making neural connections and keeping them active. Without stimuli, synaptic connections may become dormant and susceptible to pruning. The best way to keep the brain constantly engaged is to keep challenging yourself too. There are tons of things you can do along this line like taking a new route to the shopping mall, reading a mystery book, or solving a puzzle. Make it a habit to fill your day with mental stimulations.

Remember how a three year old would always ask why? It may sound silly but you can go back to being a three year old and start asking 'why' about everything you come across. This will heighten your own curiosity while at the same time keep your brain engaged.

Always Have A Positive Outlook On Life

Never get bogged down by stress or anxiety. Either one of them has been proven to kill your neurons large scale and prevent the generation of new brain cells as well. Instead, you should always think positively . You have to continuously and conscientiously replace negative thoughts with positive thinking . Keeping a positive outlook will not only dramatically relieve stress and anxiety but will also speed up the creation of new brain cells.

Make Sure That You Get Enough Sleep At Night

Improving your sleep is one of the best ways to boost your brain power. Loss of sleep results in brain degeneration. On the other hand, having enough sleep will improve your focus, your mood, your attention, your memory retention, and most important of all your thinking ability.

Drink One Cup of Coffee A Day

According to a study, drinking an 8 oz. cup of coffee improves your short term memory and enhances your attention. As a natural stimulant, coffee can energize the sympathetic nervous system. This is the part of the brain that is responsible for cognitive functioning. Coffee is also loaded with antioxidants that can help your neurons to recover from injury and stress.

Stop Smoking

Smoking decreases your cognitive ability. The carbon monoxide and free radicals in the cigarette smoke can also reach your brain and suffocate your neurons by denying them the much needed oxygen. Aside from promoting brain cell degeneration, smoking also exposes you to the risk of cerebro-vascular diseases not to mention cancer.

Write Everything By Hand

Most people nowadays prefer to type on a keyboard rather than write by hand - for convenience and efficiency not to mention precious time saved. What we do not realize however is writing by hand allows the brain to process the information more effectively and retains the knowledge in memory longer. Aside from this, the finger movements related to hand writing activate large portions of the brain particularly the regions that are identified with thinking, language, and memory.

So whenever you can, avoid using the keyboard and take out a pen and paper instead.

Be Wary of What You Eat

The food you eat can gravely impact brain plasticity and affect your cognitive abilities. For example, junk foods high in sugar and saturated fats will not only hinder the production of new neurons but will also diminish your cognitive efficiency. On the other hand, eating food rich in brain nutrients like creatine will help increase fluid intelligence. Do some research and find out the best brain food you can eat.

Conclusion

The main goal of this guide was to give you the knowledge and information that you needed to help you on the path to supercharge your brain and to use it to its greatest potential.

Not only have you learned a variety of techniques and tricks that you can use to do just that, but now you have also learned how to improve the overall quality of your life in the long run.

So, what is left for you now? The plan now is to apply everything you learned and to use these hack to turn yourself into a superhuman by supercharging your mind. Of course in the end this choice is completely up to you to make. So, ask yourself this: are you ready to begin supercharging your mind or are you just going to remain stuck in your regular and boring life?

Remember, the choice is yours to make. Good luck!

About Us

The Thought Flame is committed to add value to its customers through various books, online courses and other resources. You can learn more about us and our books at www.thethoughtflame.com.

Don't forget to check out our amazing **online video courses** at www.thethoughtflame.com/courses/ to take your knowledge to another level.

To check out our **extraordinary collection of diet/cookbooks**, visit http://www.thethoughtflame.com/category/non-fictional/cookbooks/ .

As a part of our valued relationship with our customers, we keep providing you free promotional books, courses and other stuff on subscribing with us on our site. We have a strict anti-spam policy and assure you no spam mails will be sent to your mailbox.

To subscribe with us, visit www.thethoughtflame.com.

Like our work and would like to say thanks? Buy us a cup of coffee at www.thethoughtflame.com/coffee/

Author

Amarpreet Singh is an avid learner and his passion for education has made him travel, work and study all across the world. He holds three masters degrees, including MBA, from top universities in Asia.

He is author of dozens of books, many of which are Amazon's bestseller, varying in various topics and categories. He also teaches many online courses having thousands of students across the world.

He has a keen interest in international affairs, economics, global poverty and politics, financial markets and entrepreneurship, and strives to be part of a community that shares the same passion.

He has worked as consultant with organizations like Airbus and The World Bank.

He loves travelling and learning about new cultures, and has been fortunate to live/work/travel/study in countries like India, China, Korea, US, South Africa, Japan, Philippines, Singapore, Canada etc., and learn about the culture and lifestyle in each of them.

To check out more of his work, visit www.thethoughtflame.com

www.ingramcontent.com/pod-product-compliance
Lightning Source LLC
Chambersburg PA
CBHW030532290526
45786CB00004B/1694